Gift of

The John W. Bowman Family
in memory of
Timothy Dillon Bowman

Daumier

DRAWINGS

K. E. Maison

Daumier
DRAWINGS

NEW YORK · THOMAS YOSELOFF · LONDON

© 1960 by Sagamore Press, Inc.
Library of Congress Catalog Card Number: 60-7495

Thomas Yoseloff Ltd.
123 New Bond Street
London W. 1, England

Printed in the United States of America

FOR STEFANIE

Daumier

DRAWINGS

I N HIS LIFETIME, HONORÉ DAUMIER WAS FAMOUS AS A POLITICAL AND SOCIAL satirist, and his outstanding genius as a draughtsman on the lithographic stone was readily recognized by the greatest artists and the best-known critics of his time. Delacroix as well as his arch-enemy Ingres, Courbet, and the painters of the Barbizon school, foremost among them Corot and Daubigny, admired Daumier's work greatly; critics of the standing of Balzac, Gautier, Baudelaire, and the Goncourts repeatedly praised his genius in their widely appreciated criticisms. What most of his admirers knew of Daumier's artistic activity were his lithographs, which for decades appeared regularly in *Charivari*. These lithographs were black and white impressions taken from the original drawings on stone, but as they were reproduced on cheap newsprint, the text on the reverse side frequently spoiled their beauty. Usually, only a very small number was pulled off on white paper. "Originals" of these cartoons did not exist. This was artistic journalism, the career which the young artist had chosen for himself as the only way to make a living by drawing. More than anything else he wanted to draw, and this was what he told his parents when, at the age of fourteen, he left for the second time a job his father had found for him. "Poor boy, he doesn't know what he wants to do," said his mother, and promptly the answer came: "Oh yes, I want to draw."

The able Alexandre Lenoir taught the boy the rudiments of correct drawing, imparted to him his first, lasting artistic impressions and, most important for Daumier's development, a love of sculpture. It was certainly due to Lenoir that Honoré's artistic talents were discovered. The young artist then attended an Art School, but only for a short time, and finally he joined Ramelet to learn the art of lithography. The first lithographs signed H. D. appeared in the 1820's. In the beginning, they were merely imitations of the work of more renowned lithographers but with the growing sureness of his drawing, the tenor of these lithographs became increasingly clear. Here are the beginnings of Daumier's lifelong battle against the rule of inefficient and stupid politicians, against bigotry, bureaucracy, and suppression, for the liberty of the individual, the people, and the press. In 1832, he went to prison for six months because of an anti-Louis-Philipe caricature, published the year before in *La Caricature*. It was in the lithographs which this Journal published during the few years of its existence that the real Daumier slowly emerged. Founded by Philipon, with Balzac mainly responsible for the literary part, *La Caricature* had interminable difficulties with the Censor. Twenty of its issues were seized in one year, and therefore Philipon tried to cope with his financial difficulties by issuing a special series of political lithographs, which had an extraordinary vogue at the time. In this series, edited under the title *L'Association Mensuelle,* the first true masterpieces from Daumier's hand appeared.

On Philipon's suggestion, Daumier visited several sittings of the Senate to mold in clay the faces of his paper's most prominent enemies, the parliamentarians of the Right. The actual modelling was, of course, done afterwards from memory; these

9

astonishing character studies, which were frequently used by their author for lithographs for *La Caricature,* may well have had a decisive influence on the artist's style. During the various stages of his development his drawing became more and more sculptural, and this early experience in modelling may thus have formed the basis for Daumier's very characteristic and highly personal style, which he brought to such perfection in later life.

In 1835, *La Caricature* succumbed to the wrath of the then almighty State Censorship, which forbade all political satire or caricature. Daumier now became a regular contributor to *Charivari.* His sharpened powers of observation turned to social satire and his lithographs remained the paper's main attraction for almost forty years. By 1837, the year of the popular and widely imitated *Robert Macaire* series, Daumier's fame was established.

Daumier loved to work and he loved to stroll about. He never left Paris, but lived quietly in a vast studio on the Quai d'Anjou, reading little, talking little, thinking much, smoking countless pipes, and drinking countless glasses of wine. His greatest pleasure was the company of his friends: revolutionaries, actors, painters, writers, and many of his bourgeois neighbors formed his circle. Baudelaire, who for years lived next door, was specially close to him.

About 1856, a young artist who intended to become a caricaturist, submitted some lithographs to Daumier. "Not bad" was the comment, "but why the devil, young as you are, do you want to do caricatures? I have been doing it for almost thirty years, and every time I hope it is my last one." These often quoted sentences are more than anecdote. They conceal the bitterness of a great artist who had one dominating desire in life—to be a painter—to paint instead of doing artistic journalism under contract. But he felt that he was the slave of those seven lithographic stones, always arranged on a large table in his studio. They all had to be covered with drawings, at forty francs apiece, only to come back the following week with the drawings effaced and their surfaces repolished, to be drawn on again. Often Daumier sat up late in the night to do this work so that he could paint during the day. Earlier biographers called his urge to paint *une marotte* (a folly), *une sorte de mirage, une obsession*— and an obsession it certainly was. "What would be left of Molière's work, had he been forced to live by journalism?," asks Arsène Alexandre, Daumier's first biographer, "or of Rembrandt, Teniers or Ribera, if they had been compelled to illustrate a *journal amusant?*"

Yet, Daumier had painted some masterly pictures as early as 1840-45, and he repeatedly exhibited at the Salon. The lack of public appreciation of his work never for a moment deterred him from continuing to paint. Every single picture was the result of great labors. Preparatory drawings and, frequently, painted sketches preceded it; at times the whole composition was tentatively reversed with the help of tracings. A small circle of admirers, artist friends, and a few collectors had the insight to realize the greatness of this man who was nobody's pupil and nobody's imitator. His style, in painting as well as in drawing, was completely and exclusively his own, and so was his discovery, prior to 1850, of the dissolving influence of light on form. Twenty years later, the Impressionists re-discovered this. Even the subject matter of most of Daumier's compositions was an unheard-of novelty: street scenes, proletarians, artisans, people in railway carriages, scenes from bourgeois life and the *Palais de Justice*—who had ever thought of painting these subjects without "telling stories," without charm or sentimentality, but with a deep insight into the life, the thoughts and the world of these men and women?

Daumier invariably drew from memory, *il réfléchissait d'après nature,* as a contemporary critic called it. Even portraits—and there are several—were done by heart. There is a significant story of the artist's friend Henry Monnier, to whom a portrait had been promised. Daumier was unable to bear the idea of working from a posing model and when his friend, the prospective sitter, arrived, the portrait was finished. "Superb, don't do anything more to it!" was all Monnier had to say. *C'est la certitude qui le distingue* wrote Baudelaire when he remarked on Daumier's *quasi divine* memory.

It is no doubt this sureness of the Master's touch which distinguishes even the smallest and in itself most insignificant sketches, and these Daumier drew in enormous numbers. Had he only used pen and ink as often as charcoal and black chalk, his still extant oeuvre of drawings would be larger by far. He treated his drawings with a disregard which befitted the general disorder of his studio; they were never set with fixative, but simply thrown into portfolios or boxes where pressure and friction destroyed many of them and made others fade almost beyond recognition. Naturally, the great watercolors and wash drawings which were made for sale, escaped this treatment. Especially during the years 1860-63, when Daumier had severed his relations with *Charivari,* their sale was of great importance to him, as his financial position had become most precarious. The 1860's on the other hand, were the period in the artist's life when his genius as a draughtsman was at its zenith. These are the years of the Third Class Carriages, the Amateurs, the Mountebanks, the finest of the Court Scenes, and, finally, of the Don Quixote series.

The number of his admirers steadily grew, as did his influence as an artist. Michelet, whom he had known for a long time, Millet, and Daubigny became great friends. Doré, Victor Hugo, and even Menzel, the German painter, when on a visit to Paris, were enthusiastic. When Daumier sold a painting, the price he obtained was that commanded by the work of an established artist. The American Lucas commissioned several watercolors at 200 francs each (they are now in the Walters Art Gallery in Buffalo). He lived comfortably, but very modestly, especially when in 1865 he moved to the village of Valmondois, not far from Paris. There he continued to paint and draw, and devote himself to sculpture, but he still delivered a hundred lithographs every year to *Charivari.* Soon they decreased to half that number, but those done before, during and immediately after the Franco-Prussian war of 1870-71, are of truly dramatic beauty. They were among Daumier's last works—lithographs

11

accusing those guilty of war mongering, lithographs decrying the horrors of war, and drawings of Don Quixote.

By then the Master was slowly losing his grip on life. Many of his friends were dead and he himself was fast losing his eyesight; the last six years of his life he spent in near blindness and finally in dire poverty. The State granted him a pension of 100 francs per month, just enough not to die of starvation. The last joy of his life was the knowledge that a great retrospective exhibition of his paintings and drawings was to be held at the Durand-Ruel Galleries in Paris in 1878; artist friends, some critics, and many collectors worked to assemble it. Artistically and with the press, it was a great success; financially it was a disaster.

Early in the following year, at the age of 71, Daumier died of a cerebral paralysis, thereby causing the Republic the expense of 12 francs—the cost of a Poor Man's Funeral.

Twenty four years ago a little booklet on Daumier appeared in Italy which contained a carefully compiled bibliography. Its author, G. Scheiwiller, enumerated 366 books, catalogs, and articles dealing with Daumier, quite apart from a list of books which contained woodcut illustrations by the artist. During the last decades this flood has not only continued but increased in volume. The great majority of these works, however, have one characteristic in common: they almost invariably illustrate the same paintings and drawings, the photographs of which are readily available at some Paris photographers'. The reason for this is clearly the fact that very little original research has been done on Daumier. Various authors deal with the artist's work from a literary, sociological, or revolutionist angle, others pinpoint his attitude towards Doctors, the Law, the Theater, etc., and a great number of aesthetic appreciations of a general nature keep appearing all the time. There are, however, also a few authors even at the present time, whose researches on Daumier are original and important.—I need only mention MM. Claude Roger-Marx, Cherpin, and Adhémar. Especially the latter's text in his book on Daumier (1954) is full of relevant new information.

Although it has been a relatively easy task to "shrink" Daumier's oeuvre of paintings and drawings, as represented in the voluminous catalog of the late Eduard Fuchs (1927-30), by eliminating many of that author's errors, it is by no means so easy to establish this oeuvre in its true extent. It is well known that Daumier left a great number of painted sketches which he had either discarded or not finished for one reason or another; many, perhaps even the majority of them, were later "finished," and this practice was begun at so early a date and by painters who knew the Master's technique so well that M. Adhémar may well be right in suspecting Daumier's friend and possible pupil Boulard as the earliest culprit. In contrast to more recent outright forgeries (which are more often than not copies after lesser known pictures or lithographs), the paintings which are partly by Daumier's hand present by far the most difficult problem. Similarly, many faded charcoal studies

12

were later strengthened in various ways, although there is no doubt that the artist himself on many occasions went over an earlier charcoal sketch with the pen, or sometimes with harder chalk or pencil. Plates 49, 51, and 70 are typical examples. Occasionally the student will find genuine black chalk and even pen drawings with more or less modern coloring. Worst of all, there seem to be more outright forgeries of Daumier's than of any other artist's drawings, at least as far as the nineteenth century art of France is concerned. The vast numbers of easily accessible lithographs and woodcuts were and still are for the forgers an inexhaustible source from which to copy.

Only very rarely are these forgeries dangerously clever. The great majority of them are based on the totally mistaken assumption that a Daumier drawing has to be funny, while in reality hardly one in two hundred can be called that. Witty, of course, they may well be. Copies after lithographed or wood-engraved caricatures and satires of bourgeois life are therefore predominant, while single "studies" of lawyers occur almost as frequently. The smallest group of forged drawings are the copies after important watercolors or wash drawings, but alas! even those exist in appreciable numbers.

However, the amateur of this great artist's drawings need only once acquaint himself thoroughly with their subtly individual and really inimitable style, and he will encounter little difficulty in distinguishing true from false.

LIST OF PLATES

The illustrations are not arranged in even approximately chronological order, but rather according to the subject matter of the drawings. Only a relatively small number of Daumier's drawings (which never bear a date) can be reliably dated because of their connection with lithographs or paintings the date of which is known. In a number of cases, such dates are given in the notes referring to the illustrations.

The present volume presents a selection from the material for the oeuvre catalogue which is in course of preparation. References beyond the necessary information about technique, size, and location of the drawings are therefore here dispensed with.

1 HEAD OF A BEWILDERED
  LOOKING MAN

Pen and ink. 6½ x 4¾ in. Hartford, Conn., Wadsworth Atheneum.

Daumier never tired of studying the human face and its countless varieties of expression, from blank stupidity to introspective intelligence, from delighted amusement to sheer horror, or from mild benevolence to malice. The present drawing—a fairly late example —and those illustrated on some of the following pages represent a small selection of Daumier's countless character studies. These are generally unconnected with more important compositions, either with paintings or with lithographs.

2 HEAD OF A SHOUTING MAN

Pen and wash. 3¼ x 3 in. Glasgow, Museum and Art Gallery, Burrell Collection.

3 HEAD OF A MAN

Pen and bistre wash. 5½ x 4½ in. Present location unknown.

4 HEAD OF A MAN

Pen and wash. 5¼ x 4⅛ in. Providence, R.I., John Nicholas Brown Collection.

5 A MAN STANDING AND
  LOOKING UP

Charcoal and black chalk. 6½ x 4¼ in. Present location unknown.

6 A MAN STANDING,
  HIS ARMS CROSSED

Black chalk and wash. 4⅛ x 2¾ in. Stuttgart, Staatsgalerie.

7 A MAN CROUCHING ON A STONE

Red chalk and red wash. 3⅛ x 4½ in. Formerly Berlin, Eduard Fuchs Collection.

8 THREE HEADS OF MEN

Black chalk and watercolor. 4¼ x 8½ in. New York, G. Tarnopol Collection.

Several sheets of studies of three and more heads are still preserved, but many more were probably cut up. The elaborate execution of a number of single studies of heads, on a minute scale, hardly allows for another explanation.

9 THREE STUDIES OF A MAN'S
  HEAD

Pen and wash. 5⅝ x 4 in. New York, formerly Schaeffer Gallery.

Although the three studies on this sheet are obviously of the same head, the portrait is an imaginary one; a facial type which may have fascinated Daumier when he saw it somewhere, but not a study from life. Compare plate 115.

10 STUDY OF A LAUGHING MAN

Black chalk, pen, and wash. 4¾ x 3¾ in. Cambridge, England, Fitzwilliam Museum.

11 HEAD OF A REVOLUTIONARY

Black chalk, varnished with gum arabic, laid down on board. 9 x 7 in. Paris, Private Collection.

A study for (or more likely a later repetition of) the head of the central figure in Daumier's famous painting "A Family on the Barricades," painted about 1848. The very unusual technique, unique among Daumier's drawings, conveys the impression of a cartoon rather than of a drawing.

12 STUDY OF FIVE TERROR-
  STRICKEN MEN

Pen and wash. 6¼ x 10¼ in. Paris, Maurice Gobin Collection.

13 STUDY OF FOUR MEN
(SPECTATORS)

Pen and ink. 6⅛ x 10 in. Paris, Private
Collection.

The drawing was exhibited at the Paris
Salon in 1865, but its date is neverthe-
less much earlier. The four heads of
the persons represented on this drawing also exist as individual studies.

14 STUDY OF TWO MEN
(SPECTATORS)

Pen and wash. 9½ x 7½ in. Providence,
R.I. John Nicholas Brown Collection.

15 MOTHER AND CHILD

Conté crayon. 11¾ x 9 in. Paris, César
de Hauke Collection.

16 PROFILE OF A WOMAN

Brush and sepia. 12½ x 10½ in. Paris,
Maurice Gobin Collection.

One of the very few examples of pure
brush drawing in Daumier's oeuvre.

17 THREE GOSSIPING WOMEN

Black chalk, pencil, and charcoal. 9¼ x
11½ in. Chicago, Art Institute.

This drawing as well as plate 18 is a
preliminary study for the watercolor
plate 19. The three works can safely
be dated 1852, as they are very close indeed to a lithograph published in *Charivari* on March 17 of that year.

18 THREE GOSSIPING WOMEN

Pen and ink over charcoal. 6¼ x 10¼
in. London, Victoria & Albert Museum.

19 THREE GOSSIPING WOMEN

Black chalk, pen, and watercolor. 10¼
x 7⅛ in. New York, Wildenstein Gallery.

This superb watercolor is undoubtedly
the finest of this type. Entirely un-
recorded, it was first exhibited in last
year's Daumier show at the Paris Bib-
liothèque Nationale.

20 STUDY OF A TERRIFIED WOMAN

Charcoal and pencil. 8¼ x 9¼ in. Chicago, Art Institute.

21 A WOMAN WITH HER
TWO CHILDREN

Pen and wash. 9½ x 5¾ in. Paris, Mme.
David-Weill Collection.

A variant of a subject often treated by
the artist. The composition of this
drawing, for example, appears in reverse
in the painting of a Street Scene, now
in Copenhagen.

22 A WOMAN WITH HER TWO
CHILDREN (NUDES)

Black chalk. 13¾ x 10½ in. Manchester,
Witworth Gallery.

Daumier very rarely drew Nudes; however, when he did so, he never represented the female body for the sake of
its beauty.

23 A GROUP OF NUDE WOMEN
AND A CHILD

Black chalk drawing. Size and present
location unknown. Photo Galerie Wis-
selingh, Amsterdam.

24 TWO LITTLE CHILDREN LED BY
A WOMAN (*Fragment*)

Pen and watercolor. 4⅞ x 6⅛ in. Paris,
formerly A. Schoeller Collection.

25 A PEASANT WOMAN PUTTING
BREAD INTO THE OVEN

Black chalk, slightly heightened with
white, on buff paper. 11¾ x 14¼ in.

Zürich, Collection of Frau Marianne Feilchenfeldt.

26 A WOMAN WITH THREE CHILDREN

Black chalk. 3¾ x 2¾ in. Haarlem, Holland, formerly de Bois Collection.

27 A GROUP OF LITTLE CHILDREN PLAYING

Pen and watercolor. 10⅝ x 14⅝ in. Paris, Private Collection.

The one quality Daumier lacked completely was a feeling for charm. There are certainly not more than two or three drawings—or paintings—among his works which one could call "charming;" neither are his women ever beautiful nor are his children ever delightful. Daumier must have abhorred prettiness. He probably never came nearer to creating a work of charm than he did in this and a similar group of children.

28 A BOY RUNNING

Black chalk and wash. 5⅞ x 9 in. Washington, National Gallery of Art, Rosenwald Collection.

29 MOTHERLY CARE

Tracing in black chalk. 5⅞ x 13⅜ in. London, Private Collection.

The original of this tracing was cut in half a long time ago; its right part is in a Paris Private Collection, while the left part was lost with the drawings evacuated during the last war from the print room of the Bremen Kunsthalle.

30 A BEGGAR WOMAN WITH HER TWO CHILDREN

Black chalk and wash. 7⅝ x 5⅝ in. Rotterdam, Museum Boymans — van Beuningen.

31 AT THE MARKET

Brush and sepia wash. 10 x 6¾ in. Paris, Private Collection.

A preliminary study for the more elaborate drawing in the Rockefeller Collection.

32 WOMEN WALKING WITH A CROWD

Black and red chalk and grey wash. 14⅜ x 11¾ in. Cambridge, Mass., Fogg Museum of Art.

A study connected with several larger compositions of Fugitives, of which there are several versions, datable about 1850.

33 STREET SCENE

Black chalk, pen, and watercolor. 7⅝ x 8 in. Paris, Mme. David-Weill Collection.

34 STREET SCENE

Charcoal and wash. 4⅝ x 3⅜ in. Paris, Jacques Dupont Collection.

35 "MONSIEUR, MADAME, ET BÉBÉ"

Charcoal, black chalk, and watercolor. 6¾ x 7¼ in. Paris, Private Collection.

36 THE SOUP

Charcoal, pen and wash, and watercolor, 11 x 15¾ in. Paris, Musée du Louvre.

This splendid watercolor is one of Daumier's most frequently reproduced works. The artist's range of expression is strikingly demonstrated by the contrast between the stark realism of this drawing and the almost idyllic atmosphere prevalent in the preceding one.

37 THE VERY SPECIAL BOTTLE OF WINE

Black chalk and wash and watercolor. 8¼ x 11¼ in. Stockholm, Nationalmuseum.

38 A LAST WORD

Pen and wash over black chalk. 6¾ x 8½ in. Montreal, Private Collection.

While the theme of love has never attracted Daumier, he has often treated subjects based on friendship between men. There are many studies of friends talking, walking, drinking, or looking at prints or pictures together, mostly middle-aged bourgeois at leisure—in fact the people with whom he was in daily contact.

39 GOOD FRIENDS

Composite drawing. 8⅞ x 11¾ in. Baltimore, The Maryland Institute, Lucas Collection. On loan to the Baltimore Museum of Art.

40 BEER GARDEN POLITICS

Pen and wash. 14½ x 11 in. Basle, Private Collection.

41 BATHERS

Black chalk over pencil, washed with watercolor. 8¼ x 7½ in. Baltimore, The Maryland Institute, Lucas Collection. On loan to the Baltimore Museum of Art.

42 A BLACKSMITH AT WORK

Black chalk and wash, heightened with white. 13¾ x 9⅞ in. New York, Robert Lehman Collection.

Of the three drawings treating this subject this is certainly the most important one. Jean Adhémar, in referring to the version in the Claude Roger-Marx Collection, rightly says that "this is not the study of a man making an effort, but of a person on whom a strong light is playing." The date of this and of the following drawing is probably 1857.

43 A BUTCHER AT WORK

Composite drawing. 12⅞ x 8⅞ in. Cambridge, Mass., Fogg Museum of Art.

One of several highly finished composite drawings of butchers at work. None of these splendid studies are in the least "funny," while the butchers' countenance or attitude is caricatured in all the eleven lithographs which followed the drawings during the first months of 1858. Few preliminary studies only are preserved of these subjects, but none of them was used for any of the lithographs.

44 IN THE OMNIBUS

Pen and watercolor. 4½ x 8⅞ in. Dublin, Municipal Gallery of Modern Art.

45 IN THE OMNIBUS

Charcoal, pencil, pen, and wash. 9¼ x 13⅛ in. Private Collection.

46 IN THE OMNIBUS

Black chalk and watercolor. 8¼ x 11⅞ in. Baltimore, The Walters Art Gallery.

47 IN THE OMNIBUS

Pen and black and grey wash. 7¾ x 11¾ in. Paris, Private Collection.

The finished watercolor, reproduced on the same page, has the one characteristic which is extremely rare among Daumier's drawings: it is funny. The woodcut after it, which appeared in the *Monde Illustré* in 1864, stresses this quality still further; but Daumier's true feelings speak not from the watercolor which was made for sale, but from the study for this composition.

48 THE THIRD CLASS CARRIAGE

Pen, watercolor, and gouache. 9 x 13 in. Winterthur, Dr. Oskar Reinhart Collection.

It was not until a decade or more after the introduction of railways that the public began to tire of caricatures connected with rail travel. Daumier, too, contributed many such lithographs to *Charivari;* but no caricatures are among the very numerous drawings and paintings of railway—subjects which must have occupied the artist's mind for a long time, especially in the early 1860's. The two watercolors and the preliminary studies for them here illustrated have never or only rarely been reproduced before.

49 THE THIRD CLASS CARRIAGE

Pen and wash, heightened with watercolor, over charcoal, 8¾ x 12¼ in. Zürich, Dr. L. Mohrenwitz Collection.

50 THE FIRST CLASS CARRIAGE

Black chalk and watercolor. 8 x 11¾ in. Baltimore, The Walters Art Gallery.

51 THE FIRST CLASS CARRIAGE

Charcoal, strengthened with pencil. 9 x 12¼ in. New York, E. Whye Collection.

52 MOONLIGHT LANDSCAPE

Charcoal and stump. 8¼ x 12⅛ in. Paris, Claude Roger-Marx Collection.

53 HILLY LANDSCAPE

Pen and wash. 11¾ x 16½ in. Paris, Claude Roger-Marx Collection.

Probably landscapes in the immediate vicinity of Paris, made from memory. Until his old age, Daumier was very much a city dweller and he used landscape, as a rule, only as a setting for groups of people.

54 A COUPLE CONTEMPLATING
   A LANDSCAPE

Pen and wash. 7¼ x 10½ in. Paris, formerly David-Weill Collection.

55 IN THE COUNTRY

Black chalk and watercolor. 7½ x 5½ in. Germany, Heirs of O. Gerstenberg. The only known example of a landscape drawing which the artist finished in watercolor.

56 A FAMILY IN THE COUNTRY

Pen and wash. 8¼ x 7¼ in. Germany, Heirs of O. Gerstenberg.

57 A MAN WITH HIS DOG

Black chalk and watercolor. 3¾ x 8¼ in. Present location unknown.

58 TWO PEASANTS IN
   CONVERSATION

Pen and wash. 9⅞ x 7¼ in. London, Victoria & Albert Museum.

59 STUDY OF A MAN ON HORSEBACK

Pen and ink. 8¼ x 10½ in. Paris, Claude Roger-Marx Collection.

This beautifully "flowing" and understated drawing is probably the finest among the artist's graphic representations of the horse. Daumier often watched men riding their horses into their watering-place at the Seine near his home on the Ile St. Louis, and he repeatedly painted this scene with fascinating vividness.

60 TWO HORSEMEN GALLOPING
Pen and ink. 5¾ x 11 in. Paris, Claude Roger-Marx Collection.

61 STUDY OF A MAN ON HORSEBACK

Pen and ink. 7½ x 6⅝ in. Amsterdam, Ing. van Gogh Collection.

The acquisition of this drawing by Theo van Gogh, prior to 1890, was most probably due to his brother's initiative; Vincent esteemed Daumier highly and said so repeatedly in his letters to Theo. The numerous copies, "translations into his own language," which van Gogh painted in the asylum were exclusively after originals by his few favorite painters, Rembrandt, Delacroix, Millet, and Daumier.

62 SHEET OF STUDIES WITH A GROUP OF MEN

Pencil. 16½ x 12 in. Chicago, Art Institute.

Daumier never kept sketch books, his drawings are all of different sizes, made on any piece of paper which came to hand. Tiny, very quick sketches for important paintings can not only be found in a corner of large sheets of studies, such as the two here illustrated, but also on small scraps of paper measuring just a few inches.

63 SHEET OF STUDIES

Charcoal, black chalk, and pen and ink. c. 14 x 10 in. Present location unknown.

64 STREET SINGERS

Composite drawing. 13⅜ x 10¼ in. Paris, Petit Palais.

One of the most meticulously finished of Daumier's *grande aquarelles* reproduced in almost every book on the artist, and hardly ever seen in the original. Around the middle of the 1850's Daumier seems to have taken a special interest in the representation of men and women in the act of singing. A few

examples of drawings of this kind are illustrated on this and the following plates; there are also several paintings of great beauty depicting duet singers, street serenaders, trios, etc.

65 A GUITARIST

Pen and ink over charcoal. 12 x 5⅞ in. Oxford, Private Collection.

66 A VIOLINIST

Pen and wash. 11¼ x 8⅛ in. Glasgow, Art Gallery and Museum, Burrell Collection.

This drawing exists in three very similar versions, though one of them might have been destroyed in Germany during the war.

67 TWO SINGERS

Pen and ink, slightly washed. 4⅞ x 10¼ in. Stuttgart, Staatsgalerie.

The inscriptions, although very apt, are not by Daumier.

68 A SINGER

Pen and ink. 5⅞ x 5⅛ in. New York, Hugo Moser Collection.

69 THE STREET SINGER

Black chalk (or lithographic crayon) and stump. 9 x 10⅝ in. St. Louis, Missouri, City Art Museum.

A rare example of Daumier's very polished style of drawing of a date certainly not later than 1845-50. However carefully the composition seems to have been built up, Daumier never came back to it later, when treating the same subject in the same or any other medium.

70 A PAGE PLAYING THE MANDOLIN

Black chalk over pen and wash. 12¾ x 8½ in. London, British Museum.

The unusually strong black chalk strokes which outline the main parts of the figure were probably applied by the artist himself before he repeated the composition as a painting (in the collection of the late Ed. Fuchs).

71 A CLOWN AND A DRUMMER

Charcoal, pencil, and pen and ink. 16 x 14¼ in. Rotterdam, Museum Boymans-van Beuningen.

This rather big drawing as well as the two small sketches illustrated on the same page, are preliminary studies for the watercolor reproduced on the following page (plate 24).

72 A CLOWN

Pen and wash. 5⅜ x 3½ in. Formerly in a German Private Collection.

73 A CLOWN AND A DRUMMER

Pen and wash. 4⅛ x 3¾ in. Paris, Jean Diéterle Collection.

74 A CLOWN AND A DRUMMER

Black chalk and watercolor. 14 x 10¼ in. New York, Metropolitan Museum of Art.

It has often been suggested—and not implausibly so—that the very numerous drawings and paintings of Fair Ground subjects which Daumier created between 1865 and 1870 may stem from a bitter parallel with his own life: for decades it had been his task to make the Parisians laugh at his satires and caricatures in *Charivari*, whether he felt like it or not—and, indeed he very rarely did feel like it. In a similar way, his clowns and fair ground "attractions," the Thin Woman and the Colossus, the wrestlers and the acrobats, are far from being comical or funny; often, on the contrary, they are tragic figures, their laughter is a grimace and their joyful invitation to the public—which is never shown—is purely professional.

75 MOUNTEBANKS ON THE MOVE

Pen, red chalk, and black wash. 17 x 13 in. Paris, Private Collection.

A study for the composite drawing plate 77.

76 MOUNTEBANKS ON THE MOVE

Impression (contre-épreuve) of the drawing plate 77, in red chalk, worked over in black chalk. 14½ x 10¼ in. Paris, Private Collection.

Daumier very frequently made use of the contre-épreuve technique, presumably for the purpose of deciding whether a drawing might look better in reverse, or simply to have a record of it.

77 MOUNTEBANKS ON THE MOVE

Composite drawing. 14⅜ x 10¾ in. Hartford, Conn., Wadsworth Atheneum. The most frequently exhibited drawing by Daumier, and therefore the one which is most widely known, especially in the United States.

78 A WEIGHT LIFTER

Black chalk. 9⅝ x 7⅜ in. Vienna, Albertina.

79 A WRESTLER

Charcoal. 14⅜ x 10½ in. German Private Collection.

80 THE CONJURER

Pen and wash. 4¼ x 6¼ in. Author's Collection.

81 FOUR STUDIES OF WRESTLERS

Black chalk. 8⅛ x 7 in. Paris, Formerly Marcel Guérin Collection.

These studies were used for the group of two wrestlers in the background of the painting "Les Lutteurs," in Copenhagen.

82 MOUNTEBANK PLAYING THE DRUM

Pen and watercolor. 14 x 10 in. Paris, César de Hauke Collection.

The grim figure of a juggler or conjurer who vainly tries to attract an audience to his performance by beating the drum, appears several times in Daumier's *grandes aquarelles* of the Fair Ground. A dramatic composition, in which the loneliness of the hardworking man in the shabby clothes of a clown is further stressed by the indication of a milling crowd in the background. The most meticulously finished and certainly one of the most beautiful of the artist's drawings of this kind.

83 THE THIN WOMAN AND THE COLOSSUS

Pen and watercolor. 16½ x 12⅝ in.

Esnault-Pelterie Collection, Philadelphia Museum of Art.

84 A MOUNTEBANK AND HIS FAMILY

Pen and watercolor. 13 x 15¾ in. London, Victoria & Albert Museum.

Datable about 1868, as are the two preceding drawings, this watercolor, together with a few other drawings, was acquired by the Anglo-Greek Collector Ionides from Daumier in 1878, shortly before the aged and blind artist's death.

85 THE PARADE OF THE TRAVELLING SHOW

Pen, black chalk, and watercolor. 10½ x 14½ in. Paris, Musée du Louvre.

One of several versions of this well known composition. A very small study in oil of the center figure of the barker has recently come to light and is now in the Collection of Mr. Philip Hofer.

86 PIERROT AND COLOMBINE

Pen and ink over charcoal. 16½ x 11¾ in. Rotterdam, Museum Boymans-van Beuningen.

87 STUDY FOR A SCENE FROM MOLIERE

Pen and ink, partly washed. 5¼ x 6¼ in. Geneva, Private Collection.

One of a pair of similar studies, inscribed by Arsène Alexandre, Daumier's first biographer.

88 MOUNTEBANKS RESTING

Black and red chalk over charcoal. 11¾ x 9⅞ in. Paris, Me Maurice Loncle Collection.

89 COLOMBINE BETWEEN PIERROT AND HARLEQUIN

Pen and ink over black chalk. 4¾ x 4 in. Paris, Léon Suzor Collection.

90 ACTOR WITH A TAMBOURINE

Black chalk. 16⅛ x 11 in. Minneapolis, Minnesota, Richard S. Davis Collection.

It is very typical of Daumier's later style of drawing in black chalk or charcoal to understate the drawing of the body and pay special attention to the facial expression.

91 HENRY MONNIER AS "JOSEPH PRUDHOMME"

Black chalk, pen, and wash. 16⅜ x 11⅝ in. Rotterdam, Museum Boymans-van Beuningen.

The artist, actor and author Henry Monnier, a friend of Daumier's, published his "Memoirs de Joseph Prudhomme" in 1857. This may well be the approximate date of the drawing.

92 STUDY OF A MOUNTEBANK OR ACTOR

Black chalk and wash. 8¼ x 5⅛ in. Caracas, Venezuela, Private Collection.

93 STUDY OF AN ACTOR

Pen and wash. 9½ x 6¼ in. New York, Emery Reves Collection.

A late and most powerful pen drawing, made without any preparation in black chalk or charcoal. The same unusual technique, with large areas of black wash treatment, was used for the Study of a Laughing Man, at Cambridge (plate 10).

94 ACTORS IN A SCENE FROM A TRAGEDY

Pen and wash. 5¼ x 8¼ in. Rotterdam, Museum Boymans-van Beuningen.

95 ACTORS IN A SCENE FROM A COMEDY

Pencil. 8 x 8¼ in. Paris, Claude Roger-Marx Collection.

The excellent study by M. Cherpin on *Daumier et la Théâtre* (Paris 1958) traces the artist's connection with the theater back to a very early period in his artistic life. In fact, Daumier's father Jean—Baptiste, a glazier and framer by profession and the author of many tragedies and dramas, must have maddened his helpless family by his unending declamations of poetry and drama at all times of the day. Honoré's early and persistent tendency to caricature recitations of classic verse by putting it into the mouth of ridiculous-looking actors may well stem from his youthful experiences. Daumier's numerous drawings, watercolors, and paintings of the stage and the theater, however, were not made for the purpose of amusing anybody. They are proof of his genuine love of the stage as well as of his preoccupation with the artistic possibilities he saw in the observation of an enraptured audience. Several of the well-known actors of the day were friends of Daumier's and he had free access not only to all performances at more than one theater, but also to the wings and backstage. It was very likely from that vantage point that his scrutinizing eye caught many of the impressions he later brought to paper in his drawings.

96 CHARACTERS FROM A MOLIÉRE PLAY

Black chalk and grey watercolor. 6⅛ x 9 in. Glasgow, Museum and Art Gallery, Burrell Collection.

97 "LE MALADE IMAGINAIRE"

Pen and wash. 9½ x 11¾ in. New York, Collection of Miss Edith Wetmore.

98 "LE MALADE IMAGINAIRE"

Black chalk and watercolor. 9 x 11½ in. London, Home House Trust, Courtauld Institute of Art.

99 DEATH AND THE DOCTORS

Charcoal, slightly washed. 15 x 9½ in. Private Collection.

A study closely connected with the watercolor illustrated on the following plate.

100 DEATH AND THE TWO DOCTORS

Pen and watercolor. 12¾ x 11 in. Winterthur, Dr. Oskar Reinhart Collection.

An illustration of a scene from a La

Fontaine story which ends with an argument between the two doctors. One of them emphatically declares that the patient would still be alive if only his advice had been heeded, while the other had "foreseen it all."

101 THREE ATTENTIVE
SPECTATORS

Pen and watercolor. 4 x 4¾ in. Present location unknown.

102 THREE BORED SPECTATORS

Pen and ink. 4⅜ x 5½ in. Paris, Pierre Granville Collection.

103 THE INTERVAL

Composite drawing. 9⅝ x 13. Winterthur, Dr. Oskar Reinhart Collection.

104 STUDY OF SPECTATORS

Pen and ink. 4½ x 8 in. Rotterdam, Museum Boymans-van Beuningen.

105 THE CRITICS IN THE THEATER

Pen and watercolor. 10½ x 14 in. Lost. Formerly Berlin, Gerstenberg Collection.

This title, under which the watercolor was exhibited for the last time in 1926, appears to be very appropriate: the two habitués in the center of the front row are obviously the only spectators in a laughing crowd who have decided to reserve their judgment—they are not so easily amused. A masterly drawing, the loss of which is much to be regretted.

106 A BOX IN THE THEATER

Pen and watercolor. 7½ x 10⅝ in. Paris, Ernest Rouart Collection.

Stylistically and technically a very unusual drawing in Daumier's oeuvre.

M. Adhémar very rightly comments on the resemblance of Manet's pastel portraits of women to the treatment of the profiles in this watercolor. It is, of course, quite possible that Manet knew this study or the one illustrated by plate 16.

107 THE WATCH BY THE
DEATH BED

Pen and ink. 9⅛ x 11⅜ in. Zürich, Collection of Frau Marianne Feilchenfeldt.

A satirical drawing, bordering on caricature, of which two very similar versions are known.

108 DEATH AND THE DOCTOR

Black chalk over charcoal. 6¼ x 9¾ in. Paris, formerly Michel-Lévy Collection.

109 A MAN READING ALOUD

Black chalk and charcoal. 9½ x 11¾ in. Rotterdam, Museum Boymans-van Beuningen.

110 THE READER

Black chalk. 5¾ x 8 in. Paris, formerly Fix-Masson Collection.

111 STUDY OF A MAN
LISTENING TO MUSIC

Pen and ink. 14¾ x 13⅛ in. Rotterdam, Museum Boymans-van Beuningen.

It is a remarkable characteristic of Daumier that he was, it seems, invariably fascinated by the attitude and facial expression of people whose attention was focussed on some passive task, like being read to, listening to music, or looking at pictures. The studies of spectators and even those of silent and patient railroad travellers are of the same category.

112 SKETCH OF A MAN PLAYING THE PIANO

Pen and ink. 9½ x 11⅞ in. Paris, Claude Roger-Marx Collection.

113 THE MUSIC LOVER

Pen and wash over charcoal and stump. 11⅜ x 9 in. Lost. Formerly Berlin, Gerstenberg Collection.

Here again, as in the case of plate 105, this most beautiful composition of the series became a war casualty.

114 A PAINTER AT WORK

Composite drawing. 7¾ x 7¼ in. United States, Private Collection.

115 AN AMATEUR INSPECTING A PAINTING

Pen and wash. 5¼ x 4½ in. New York, G. Tarnopol Collection.

Compare the drawing to plate 9.

116 A PAINTER CONTEMPLATING HIS WORK

Pen and brown wash. 15 x 11⅜ in. Paris, Comte de Gramont Collection.

It has been suggested that this drawing represents the Barbizon painter Charles Daubigny, who was a close friend of Daumier's.

117 AN ARTIST SHOWING HIS DRAWINGS TO A COLLECTOR

Pen and watercolor. 7 x 9½ in. Winterthur, Dr. Oskar Reinhart Collection.

Although there are a number of drawings and paintings of artists' studios among Daumier's works, the world of collectors of prints and drawings fascinated him far more. Many paintings, drawings, and lithographs, mostly of the 1860's show the passionate collector either quietly enjoying the possession of his treasures or showing them to friends and "rivals." In some well-known pictures and water-colors—and in the studies for them—the collectors are seen looking for "finds" in exhibitions, previews of auction sales, or outside dealers' shops.

118 THE PRINT COLLECTOR

Black chalk, pen, and ink. 13 x 10 in. Zürich, Collection of Frau Marianne Feilchenfeldt.

A study for the well-known painting "L'Amateur d'Estampes" which exists in more than two versions, the finest in Philadelphia and in the Paris Petit Palais. A similar study is in the Claude Roger-Marx Collection.

119 THE CONNOISSEURS

Black chalk, wash, and watercolor, 9¾ x 7¼ in. Cleveland, Ohio, The Museum of Art.

The scene is the Hôtel des Ventes, or the Hôtel Drouot, Paris' main center for auction sales. A much less subtle version of this widely reproduced drawing appeared in the form of a satirical woodcut in *Le Monde Illustré* in 1863.

120 THE TWO PRINT COLLECTORS

Black chalk, pen, and watercolor. 13¾ x 12⅝ in. London, Victoria & Albert Museum.

121 THE AMATEUR

Black chalk, wash, and watercolor. 17⅜ x 13¾ in. New York, Metropolitan Museum of Art.

One of Daumier's most important watercolors made for sale, well planned by preparatory studies, meticulously finished, and on a very big scale. In the same way as in the drawing illustrated on the opposite page (plate 120), the calm and secluded atmosphere of the collector's study prevails, and the impression is conveyed that these men have no other interest in life beside their collections.

122 AT THE ART EXHIBITION

Pen, red chalk, charcoal, and sepia wash. 5⅞ x 5½ in. Paris, R. Delapalme Collection.

123 THREE AMATEURS AT AN EXHIBITION

Pen and sepia wash. 4¼ x 5⅛ in. Providence, R.I., Rhode Island School of Design.

124 A MOMENT'S REST AT THE ART EXHIBITION

Charcoal and black chalk. 6⅛ x 8½ in. Copenhagen, Ordrupgaard, Hansen Collection.

The drawing is similar in conception to a woodcut which appeared in the *Monde Illustré* in May 1868, on the occasion of the great *Exposition des Beaux-Arts.*

125 SKETCH FOR "LES AMATEURS DE TABLEAUX"

Charcoal and watercolor. 4½ x 3½ in. Paris, Jacques Dupont Collection.

A quickly drawn first study for the well-known picture, followed by a painted sketch with the figures half-length, and by two similar final versions of the composition.

126 STUDY FOR A LAWYER ON THE DEFENSE

Pen and ink over charcoal. 10⅝ x 6⅞ in. Paris, Maurice Gobin Collection.

127 STUDY FOR A LAWYER ON THE ATTACK

Pen and ink over charcoal. 10⅝ x 8¼ in. Paris, Maurice Gobin Collection.

The two drawings illustrated side by side originally formed one sheet. Both are studies for the two lawyers in the magnificent watercolor plate 139.

128 STUDY FOR A PLEADING LAWYER

Pen and wash over charcoal. 10½ x 7⅜ in. Paris, Mᵉ Loncle Collection.

129 TWO LAWYERS IN CONVERSATION

Composite drawing. 9⅞ x 8⅝ in. Paris, Georges Lévy Collection.

A splendid drawing, datable about 1860, which has only recently come to light.

130 IN THE CORRIDORS OF THE PALAIS DE JUSTICE

Black chalk and watercolor. 8⅝ x 6⅜ in. Reims, Musée.

Probably not later than 1860. This subtle character study was bequeathed to the Reims Museum more than fifty years ago, but it has only once been reproduced in a small booklet on Daumier, in 1935, having otherwise escaped the attention of all the artist's biographers.

131 STUDY OF FOUR LAWYERS

Pen and wash. 10½ x 9½ in. Chicago, Leigh B. Block Collection.

The only one of the more important late compositions of this kind drawn in this technique and without any preparation in charcoal or black chalk.

132 LAWYERS AWAITING THE OPENING OF THE DOORS

Pen and watercolor, heightened with white bodycolor. 5⅞ x 9¼ in. Winterthur, Dr. Oskar Reinhart Collection.

133 LAWYERS AWAITING THE OPENING OF THE DOORS

Pen and watercolor. 6¼ x 8½ in. New York, Mrs. Charles R. Henschel Collection.

Two fine watercolors treating the same subject in essentially the same medium. The drawing in Winterthur (plate 132), with its very subtle white highlights, is probably the later one, though both must be close to 1860.

134 A PLEADING LAWYER

Pen and watercolor. 6⅜ x 8⅝ in. New York, Formerly Jakob Goldschmidt Collection.

135 A PLEADING LAWYER

Pen and watercolor. 7½ x 11⅝ in. Paris, Private Collection.

Almost all Daumier's Court Scenes and even the numerous sketches of pleading lawyers and somnolent judges have the same theme: they are pungent satires on the hypocrisy of legal procedure and its exponents. Two practically identical versions exist of this drawing, one of them having been made with the help of a tracing; this latter is still preserved in the Museum Boymans-van Beuningen, Rotterdam.

136 STUDY FOR "HUIS CLOS"

Pen and ink, with traces of charcoal. 8 x 13⅛ in. Paris, Me Loncle Collection.

137 "HUIS CLOS" (THE TESTIMONY BEHIND CLOSED DOORS)

Pen, wash, and gouache. 8½ x 13⅜ in. Copenhagen, Ny Carlsberg Glyptotek.

138 STUDY OF TWO LAWYERS IN COURT

Pen and wash. 9⅝ x 15½ in. Private Collection.

Very likely a first sketch for the composition of the watercolor reproduced below (plate 139). For studies of the two lawyers, see the drawings plates 126 and 127.

139 "A FAMOUS CASE"

Pen and watercolor. 10¼ x 17 in. Esnault-Pelterie Collection, Philadelphia Museum of Art.

140 A LAWYER READING A DOCUMENT TO THE TRIBUNAL

Black chalk and wash. About 11 x 15 in. Basle, Private Collection.

A smaller but more carefully finished watercolor of the same subject is in the Collection of Dr. Oskar Reinhart, Winterthur; although its composition is considerably simplified, the drawing here illustrated is undoubtedly the study for it.

141 THE SPEECH FOR THE DEFENSE

Black chalk, wash, and watercolor. 10⅜ x 14⅜ in. Lost. Formerly Berlin, Gerstenberg Collection.

This subject is treated in a series of very beautiful drawings. In contrast to most other court scenes, the decisive figure is perhaps less the defending lawyer than the client or his friend or relative: he may be smiling at the barrister's hypocrisy, or listening to some last-minute advise (or giving it) or, as in this dramatic drawing, anxiously listening to the speech on which everything might depend for his son or friend.

142 DON QUIXOTE AND SANCHO PANZA IN THE MOUNTAINS

Charcoal. 3¾ x 6¾ in. Private Collection.

The Don Quixote illustrations now reproduced in these last pages represent a selection only from a fairly extensive group of such drawings. They are, in fact, among Daumier's last drawings and some of them may be as late at 1870-71, the time of his last political satires during and immediately after the Franco-Prussian War. While he was carrying on his vain fight against war and Imperialism, as he had earlier fought an unending battle against stupidity, hypocrisy, and oppression, Daumier again took to one of the favorite subjects of his later years, the story of Don Quixote. The parallel could not possibly have escaped him.

143 DON QUIXOTE AND SANCHO PANZA

Pen and ink over charcoal. 7⅝ x 9 9/8 in. Paris, Claude Roger-Marx Collection.

A study for the two paintings in the London National Gallery and in the Payson Collection, New York.

144 SANCHO AND HIS DONKEY

Pen and wash. 5½ x 5 in. New York, Richard Sisson Collection.

145 SANCHO BEHIND A TREE

Pen and wash. 10⅜ x 14⅝ in. New York, E. M. Remarque Collection.

146 DON QUIXOTE AND SANCHO PANZA IN THE COUNTRY

Black chalk and watercolor. 5½ x 10⅜ in. Paris, Private Collection.

This fine watercolor may well have been the greatest commercial success among Daumier's Don Quixote compositions, of which three almost identical versions are already known to the present author, while more are likely to exist. Mr. Erich Maria Remarque possesses a large painted version.

147 STUDY OF DON QUIXOTE AND SANCHO

Black chalk and wash. 6¼ x 8⅝ in. New York, Metropolitan Museum of Art.

148 DON QUIXOTE TURNING SOMERSAULTS IN FRONT OF SANCHO

Charcoal. 13⅜ x 9⅞ in. Winterthur, Dr. Oskar Reinhart Collection.

149 DON QUIXOTE AND SANCHO PANZA IN THE MOUNTAINS

Charcoal on brownish paper. 5¾ x 9 in. Crystal Bay, Minnesota, Mr. and Mrs. Richard S. Davis Collection.

150 DON QUIXOTE BY MOONLIGHT
Charcoal. 7⅝ x 10⅜ in. Basle, Robert von Hirsch Collection.

PLATES

1 Head of a Bewildered Looking Man

2 Head of a Shouting Man

3 Head of a Man

4 Head of a Man

5 A Man Standing and Looking Up

6 A Man Standing, His Arms Crossed

7 A Man Crouching on a Stone

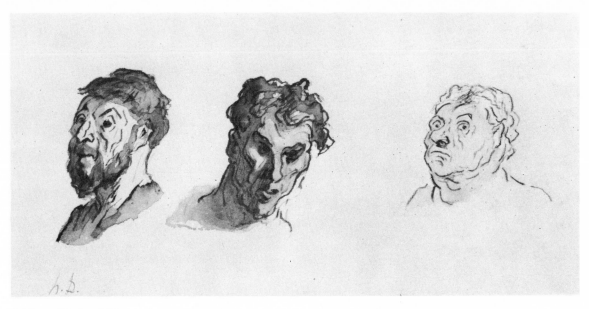

8 Three Heads of Men

9 Three Studies of a Man's Head

10 Study of a Laughing Man

11 Head of a Revolutionary

12 Study of Five Terror-Stricken Men

13 Study of Four Men (Spectators)

14 Study of Two Men (Spectators)

15 Mother and Child

16 Profile of a Woman

17 Three Gossiping Women

18 Three Gossiping Women

19 Three Gossiping Women

20 Study of a Terrified Woman

21 A Woman with Her Two Children

22 A Woman with Her Two Children (Nudes)

23 A Group of Nude Women and a Child

24 Two Little Children Led by a Woman (*Fragment*)

25 A Peasant Woman Putting Bread into the Oven

26 A Woman with Three Children

27 A Group of Little Children Playing

28 A Boy Running

29 Motherly Care

30 A Beggar Woman with Her Two Children

31 At the Market

32 Women Walking with a Crowd

33 Street Scene

34 Street Scene

35 "Monsieur, Madame, et Bébé"

36 The Soup

37 The Very Special Bottle of Wine

38 A Last Word

39 Good Friends

40 Beer Garden Politics

41 Bathers

42 A Blacksmith at Work

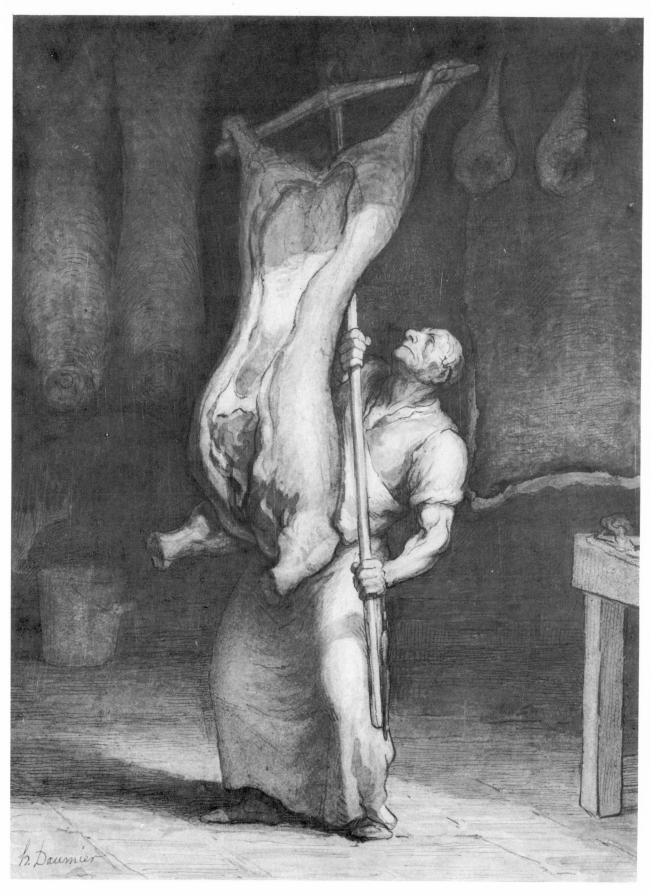

43 A Butcher at Work

44 In the Omnibus

45 In the Omnibus

46 In the Omnibus

47 In the Omnibus

48 The Third Class Carriage

49 The Third Class Carriage

50 The First Class Carriage

51 The First Class Carriage

52 Moonlight Landscape

53 Hilly Landscape

54 A Couple Contemplating a Landscape

55 In the Country

56 A Family in the Country

57 A Man with His Dog

58 Two Peasants in Conversation

59 Study of a Man on Horseback

60 Two Horsemen Galloping

61 Study of a Man on Horseback

62 Sheet of Studies with a Group of Men

63 Sheet of Studies

64 Street Singers

65 A Guitarist

66 A Violinist

67 Two Singers

68 A Singer

69 The Street Singer

70 A Page Playing the Mandolin

71 A Clown and a Drummer

72 A Clown

73 A Clown and a Drummer

74 A Clown and a Drummer

75 Mountebanks on the Move

76 Mountebanks on the Move

77 Mountebanks on the Move

78 A Weight Lifter

79 A Wrestler

80 The Conjurer

81 Four Studies of Wrestlers

82 Mountebank Playing the Drum

83 The Thin Woman and the Colossus

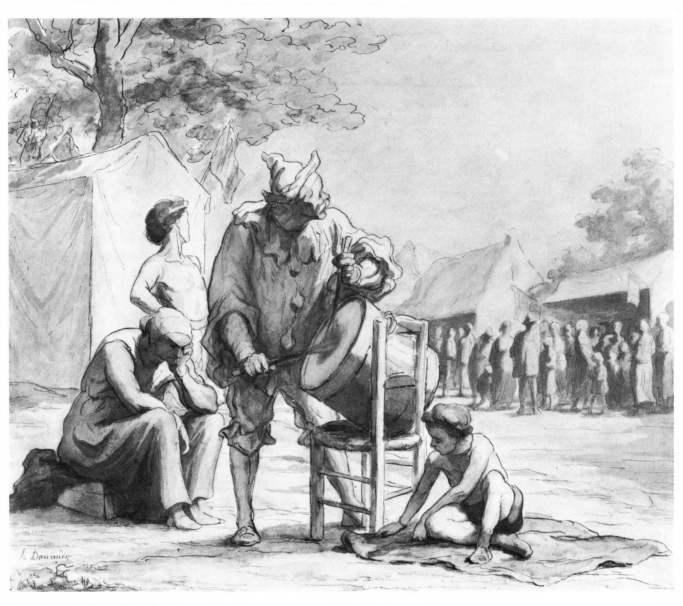

84 A Mountebank and His Family

85 The Parade of the Travelling Show

86 Pierrot and Colombine

Rechercher de personnages du théâtre de molière, par H. Daumier, provenant de son atelier de Valmondois, souvenir affectueux, d'Arsène Alexandre à son cher ami Coquelin cadet.

87 Study for a Scene from Molière

88 Mountebanks Resting

89 Colombine Between Pierrot and Harlequin

90 Actor with a Tambourine

91 Henry Monnier as "Joseph Prudhomme"

92 Study of a Mountebank or Actor

93 Study of an Actor

94 Actors in a Scene from a Tragedy

95 Actors in a Scene from a Comedy

96 Characters from a Molière Play

97 "Le Malade Imaginaire"

98 "Le Malade Imaginaire"

99 Death and the Doctors

100 Death and the Two Doctors

101 Three Attentive Spectators

102 Three Bored Spectators

103 The Interval

104 Study of Spectators

105 The Critics in the Theater

106 A Box in the Theater

107 The Watch by the Death Bed

108 Death and the Doctor

109 A Man Reading Aloud

110 The Reader

111 Study of a Man Listening to Music

112 Sketch of a Man Playing the Piano

113 The Music Lover

114 A Painter at Work

115 An Amateur Inspecting a Painting

116 A Painter Contemplating His Work

117 An Artist Showing His Drawings to a Collector

118 The Print Collector

119 The Connoisseurs

120 The Two Print Collectors

121 The Amateur

122 At the Art Exhibition

123 Three Amateurs at an Exhibition

124 A Moment's Rest at the Art Exhibition

125 Sketch for "Les Amateurs de Tableaux"

126 Study for a Lawyer on the Defense

127 Study for a Lawyer on the Attack

128 Study for a Pleading Lawyer

129 Two Lawyers in Conversation

130 In the Corridors of the Palais de Justice

131 Study of Four Lawyers

132 Lawyers Awaiting the Opening of the Doors

133 Lawyers Awaiting the Opening of the Doors

134 A Pleading Lawyer

135 A Pleading Lawyer

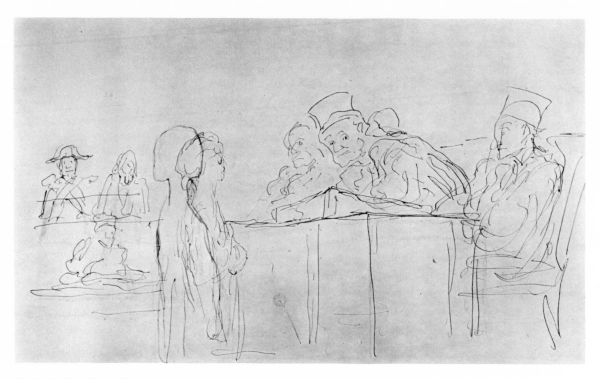

136 Study for "Huis Clos"

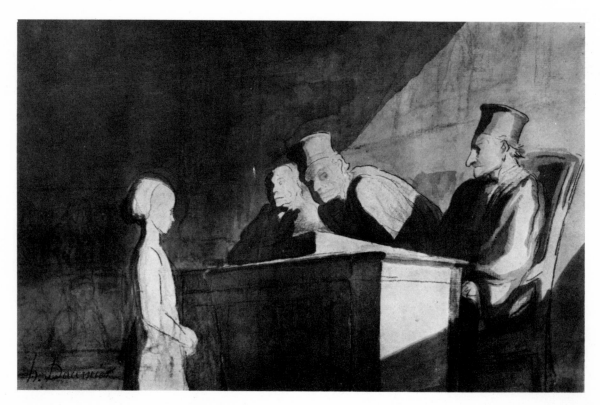

137 "Huis Clos" (The Testimony Behind Closed Doors)

138 Study of Two Lawyers in Court

139 "A Famous Case"

140 A Lawyer Reading a Document to the Tribunal

141 The Speech for the Defense

142 Don Quixote and Sancho Panza in the Mountains

143 Don Quixote and Sancho Panza

144 Sancho and His Donkey

145 Sancho Behind a Tree

146 Don Quixote and Sancho Panza in the Country

147 Study of Don Quixote and Sancho

148 Don Quixote Turning Somersaults in Front of Sancho

149 Don Quixote and Sancho Panza in the Mountains

150 Don Quixote by Moonlight